ALL TIME FAVORITE CHRISTMAS Cookies

35 Easy and Delicious, All Time Favorite
Christmas Cookie Recipes From Around the World

DISCLAIMER

Introduction

'All Time Favorite Christmas Cookies' introduces thirty-five kitchen-tested recipes to induce sugary sweet comas, happy feelings, and warm kitchen memories this holiday season. Learn to create your own traditional cookies: from lemon cookies to gingerbread men, from teacake cookies to crunchy, peppermint cookies. The variety and the ingredients of each little morsel leave these cookies unmatched!

Furthermore, take your kitchen around the world with many recipes that pulse with the vibrant energy of places like

Germany, France, Italy, and Croatia. Different places around the world are enriched with their own essential holiday spirit. Give your holiday tradition a spice of what's going on else where in the world and enjoy delicious creations such as the Croatian Christmas Medeniaci Cookies, Parisian Delight Chocolate Ganache Cookies and Merry Milano Cookies.

Understand that your holiday parties, your kid's after-school treats, and your mid-day snacks can get a whole lot more interesting during these wintery months. Grab your mixing bowl, a few simple ingredients, and drive this warmth and deliciousness into your everyday holiday schedule. This is truly the most wonderful time of the year; allow these little morsels of vibrant spiced flavor, peppermint richness, gooey chocolate, and peanut butter nuttiness to enrich your holiday spirit. And if you're all about variety, this book of 35 creative, step-by-step recipes with easy ingredients will accomplish all your cookie baking needs!

Give your loved ones the gift of holiday memory by helping them spread the (recipe-included) holiday buttercream frosting over the Holiday traditional sugar cookies; help them glitter sprinkles over the delicious cream. Furthermore, help them to understand that this time of year is the ONLY time of year it's acceptable to, yes, lick your fingers between each cookie-decorating endeavor. Nothing is so sinfully delicious as this beautiful, vibrant time of year.

This world of winter weather, of snowstorms, of glittering cookies, of warm morsels, and of gooey chocolate can be yours this holiday season. Prepare your tummy for the wild intake of flavor, and prepare yourself for bouts of earnest laughter, warm kitchen smells, and vibrant holiday parties. Enjoy yourself this year more than you ever have before. Make this holiday season one to remember. Start your own holiday tradition, today. I hope you enjoy this Holiday Season with these truly delicious all time favorite treats!

Table of Contents

Chapter 4: Holiday No-Bake Cookies 55

Chapter 5: Holidays Round-the-World Cookies 65

CHAPTER 1
HOLIDAY
Tradition Cookies

Nutcracker Tea Cakes

Recipe Makes 36 cookies.
Prep Time: 20 minutes.
Cook Time: 12 minutes.

Ingredients:
2 cups flour
1 cup butter
1 ¼ cup diced walnuts
1 tsp. vanilla
7 tbsp. confectioners' sugar

Directions:
Begin by preheating the oven to 350 degrees Fahrenheit.

Next, stir together the vanilla and the butter until the mixture is completely smooth.

To the side, mix together the confectioners' sugar and the flour. Stir the mixture together, and add this dry mixture to the butter mixture. Next, add the walnuts, and roll the mixture into small dough balls.

Place the dough balls on a baking sheet, and allow the cookies to bake for twelve minutes in the oven. Enjoy.

Classic Touch Christmas Sugar Cookies

Recipe Makes 60 cookies.
Prep Time: 20 minutes.
Cook Time: 8 minutes.

Ingredients:
1 stick of butter
1 1/3 cup white sugar
¾ cup brown sugar
2 tbsp. milk
1 tsp. vanilla
3 eggs
4 cups all-purpose flour
1 ½ tsp. cream of tartar
1 tsp. baking soda
1 tsp. salt

Frosting Ingredients:
1/3 stick butter
1 ¼ tsp. vanilla
4 cups powdered sugarBel
7 tbsp. milk
food coloring of your choice

Directions:

Begin by combining together butter, white sugar, and the brown sugar in a bowl. Add milk, eggs, and the vanilla. Continue to stir.

Next, stir together the cream of tartar, flour, baking soda, and salt in a large bowl. Bring together the wet ingredients and the dry ingredients, and stir well. Chill the dough for two hours.

Next, preheat your oven to 350 degrees Fahrenheit. Roll the dough out on a floured surface, and cut the dough out with cookie cutters—reindeer, Santa, snowflakes, etc. Place these cookies on a baking sheet, and allow them to cook for eight minutes. Make sure they cool before frosting them.

To create the frosting, stir together the vanilla, shortening, and powdered sugar. Blend the ingredients well until you reach a creamy, smooth texture.

Add this mixture overtop the cookies, and add sprinkles, if you please. Have fun, get creative, and enjoy as you go. After all: the holidays only come once a year!

Up a HootyCreek Christmas Cookie

Recipe Makes 18 cookies.
Prep Time: 25 minutes.
Cook Time: 0 minutes.

Ingredients:
1 cup all-purpose flour
½ cup oatmeal
½ tsp. baking soda
½ cup brown sugar
1/3 cup white sugar
½ tsp. salt
½ cup softened butter
1 egg
1 tsp. vanilla
½ cup diced pecans
½ cup dried cranberries
1/3 cup white chocolate chips

Directions:
Begin by preheating the oven to 350 degrees Fahrenheit.

Next, mix together the butter, egg, and vanilla. Mix until the ingredients are fluffy. To the side, mix together all the dry ingredients: flour, oatmeal, baking soda, brown sugar, white sugar, and salt.

Bring the wet ingredients and the dry ingredients together, and stir well. Add the pecans, cranberries, and white chocolate chips, and continue to stir.

Drop the cookies onto a baking sheet, and allow them to bake for ten minutes. Cool the cookies, and enjoy!

Linus and Lucy Lemon Snow Day Cookies

Recipe Makes 36 cookies.
Prep Time: 10 minutes.
Cook Time: 9 minutes.

Ingredients:
1 lemon cake mix package
1 tsp. lemon extract
2 eggs
1/3 cup vegetable oil
½ cup confectioners' sugar for sprinkling

Directions:
Begin by preheating the oven to 375 degrees Fahrenheit.

Next, pour the cake mix, eggs, oil, and the extract together in a large bowl and stir them until they're well-blended. Next, drop each of the cookies into a bowl filled with the confectioners' sugar. Allow the cookies to roll in the sugar, and then put them on a baking sheet.

Bake the cookies for nine minutes, and allow them to cool prior to enjoying.

White Chocolate Blondie Party Squares

Recipe Makes 16 bars.
Prep Time: 15 minutes.
Cook Time: 20 minutes.

Ingredients:
1 egg
1 ½ cup all-purpose flour
1 cup dried cranberries
2 cups boiling water
1 tsp. baking powder
1 cup softened butter
½ tsp. salt
1 ½ cups brown sugar
1 cup white chocolate chips
4 tsp. vanilla

Directions:
Begin by preheating the oven to 350 degrees Fahrenheit.

Next, boil the cups of water and then combine the dried cranberries with the hot water in order to completely rehydrate them. Allow them to sit together for one full minute prior to draining them.

Next, stir together the brown sugar and the butter. Best results stem from an electric mixer. Next, add the eggs and the vanilla.

To the side, in a different bowl, stir together the salt, the baking powder, and the flour. Mix this into the wet ingredient mixture slowly.

Next, add the cranberries and the white chocolate, Mix the ingredients, and then press the mixture into the bottom of a pan. Bake this blondie batter for twenty minutes, and allow them to cool prior to slicing up and enjoying.

White Winter Chocolate and Cranberry Cookies

Recipe Makes 24 cookies.
Prep Time: 15 minutes.
Cook Time: 10 minutes.

Ingredients:
1 1/3 cup all-purpose flour
½ cup softened butter
½ tsp. baking soda
¾ cup brown sugar
¼ cup white sugar
1 cup white chocolate chips
1 egg
1 tbsp. brandy
1 ¼ cup dried cranberries

Directions:
Begin by preheating your oven to 375 degrees Fahrenheit.

Next, bring together butter, white sugar, and the brown sugar. Stir well until the mixture is completely smooth. Afterwards, add the brandy and the egg and stir well. Add the flour and the baking soda, and mix in the cranberries and the white chocolate chips.

After you've sufficiently mixed the cookie dough, drop the cookies onto the baking sheet, and allow the cookies to bake for ten minutes. Allow them to cool, and enjoy!

Cashew Craving Christmas Cookies

Recipe Makes 48 cookies
Prep Time: 30 minutes.
Cook Time: 10 minutes.

Ingredients:
2 ¼ cups all-purpose flour
3 tsp. grated orange zest
1 tsp. baking powder
1 tsp. vanilla
½ tsp. baking soda
1 cup diced and salted cashews
¾ cup softened butter
6 ounces diced and dried cranberries
½ cup sour cream
1 egg
1 ½ cups confectioners' sugar
3 tbsp. orange juice

Directions:
Begin by preheating the oven to 375 degrees Fahrenheit.

Next, stir together baking powder, baking soda, and the flour in a small bowl.

To the side, mix together the butter, brown sugar, sour cream, orange zest, egg, and the vanilla. Beat the mixture until it's creamy.

Next, add the flour mixture to this wet ingredient mixture. Stir well until the dough is smooth. Add the cashews and the cranberries to the dough, and stir.

Drop the cookie-dough rounds on the baking sheet, and allow the cookies to bake for about ten minutes—until they're browned.

To the side, stir together the confectioners' sugar and the orange juice. Drizzle this created glaze over the cookies, and enjoy.

Shortbread Shimmy Holiday Cookie

Recipe Makes 24 cookies.
Prep Time: 10 minutes.
Cook Time: 15 minutes.

Ingredients:
1/3 cup cornstarch
1 cup softened butter
1 1/3 cup all-purpose flour
½ cup confectioners' sugar

Directions:
Begin by preheating the oven to 375 degrees Fahrenheit.

Next, stir together butter, cornstarch, flour, and the confectioners' sugar, using an electric mixer, if you have one. Beat them on low for one minute; afterwards, switch to high for four minutes.

Afterwards, drop the dough into 24 cookies on a baking sheet, and cook them for fifteen minutes. Cool the cookies, and enjoy.

Rockin' (Round the Christmas Tree) Peanut Butter Cookie

Recipe Makes 40 cookies
Prep Time: 25 minutes.
Cook Time: 10 minutes.

Ingredients:
2 cups all-purpose flour
½ cup brown sugar
½ tsp. salt
1 egg
1 tsp. vanilla
1 tsp. baking soda
2 tbsp. milk
½ cup softened butter
¾ cup peanut butter
½ cup white sugar
40 mini peanut butter cups, no wrapper

Directions:
Begin by preheating the oven to 375 degrees Fahrenheit.

Next, stir together baking soda, salt, and flour in one bowl. Set this bowl to the side.

In a larger bowl, stir together sugar, peanut butter, butter, and brown sugar. Mix them until they're fluffy. Add the vanilla, egg, and the milk. Next, stir in the dry ingredients and continue to stir until completely assimilated.

Shape the dough into one-inch balls, and place them on a baking pan. Bake the cookies for eight minutes. Afterwards, press the mini peanut butter cup into each of the cookies immediately, and allow the cookies to cool. After they've cooled, enjoy!

Raspberry Almond Cindy Lou-Hoo Cookies

Recipe Makes 36 cookies.
Prep Time: 30 minutes.
Cook Time: 18 minutes.

Ingredients:
2 cups flour
½ cup confectioners' sugar
1 cup softened butter
1 cup white sugar
1 ½ tsp. almond extract
1 tsp. milk
½ cup raspberry jam

Directions:
Begin by preheating the oven to 350 degrees Fahrenheit.

Next, mix together white sugar, butter, and one tablespoon of the almond extract. Add the flour and stir until the dough begins to stick together. Roll the dough into small balls, and place them on a cookie sheet. Position a tiny indent in the center of the cookies, and place a dot of raspberry jam in each hole.

Allow the cookies to bake for eighteen minutes.

To the side, mix together ½ tsp. of almond extract, the confectioners' sugar, and the milk. Stir until the mixture is completely smooth. Afterwards, drizzle this mixture overtop of the already baked cookies.

Enjoy!

Peanut Butter Delight Noel Bars

Recipe Makes 16 bars.
Prep Time: 25 minutes.
Cook Time: 90 minutes.

Ingredients:
1 cup smooth peanut butter
1 cup melted butter
1 ½ cups chocolate chips
2 ½ cups graham cracker crumbs
4 tbsp. additional peanut butter
2 cups confectioners' sugar

Directions:
Begin by mixing together confectioners' sugar, melted butter, graham cracker crumbs, and the first cup of peanut butter. Stir until it's completely assimilated. Next, press the mixture into a 9x13 inch pan.

Next, stir together the chocolate chips and the 4 tbsp. of peanut butter in a microwave-safe bowl. Allow the mixture to melt in the microwave, stirring the mixture occasionally until it's completely melted.

Spread this mixture over the created crust, and allow the peanut butter bars to refrigerate for one hour prior to enjoying.

CHAPTER 2
HOLIDAY
Tradition Peppermint Cookies

Peppermint Chocolate Cookie Sandwiches

Recipe Makes 18 cookies.
Prep Time: 25 minutes.
Cook Time: 8 minutes.

Ingredients:
2 ½ cups bittersweet chocolate baking chips
2 eggs
2 tbsp. butter
¼ cup flour
1 cup sugar
1 tsp. vanilla
½ tsp. baking powder

Filling:
8 ounces softened cream cheese
1 tbsp. milk
1 cup powdered sugar
1 peppermint bark baking bar

Directions:
Begin by preheating your oven to 350 degrees Fahrenheit.

Next, mix together one cup of the chocolate chips and the butter in a saucepan, and allow them to melt together slowly on low heat. Remove the saucepan from the heat, and add flour, sugar, eggs, vanilla, and baking powder. Beat the mixture completely, and add the rest of the chocolate chips.

Next, drop the dough onto a baking sheet, and bake the cookies for eight minutes. Allow them to cool completely on a wire rack.

Next, stir together cream cheese, milk, powdered sugar, and the chopped-up baking bar. Spread this filling over one half of the cookie bottoms, and place an additional cookie overtop. Enjoy your cookie sandwiches!

Sunny Snowball Candy Cane Cookies

Recipe Makes 60 cookies.
Prep Time: 20 minutes.
Cook Time: 20 minutes.

Ingredients:
1 cup diced pecans
2 cups softened butter
1/3 cup crushed candy canes
1 cup confectioners' sugar
1 tsp. vanilla
3 ½ cups all-purpose flour
8 ounces chopped white confectioners' coating

Directions:
Begin by beating together the confectioners' sugar and the butter in a large bowl until it's creamy. Add the vanilla and the flour, and continue to beat to create dough. Add the pecans, and stir well before refrigerating for four hours.

Next, preheat your oven to 350 degrees Fahrenheit. Roll this dough into one-inch balls and bake the cookies for twenty minutes. Remove them from the oven, and allow them to cool.

Next, crush up the candy canes in a shallow bowl. To the side, microwave the confectioners' coating in a small bowl for thirty seconds. Afterwards, stir the coating. Cook it for fifteen seconds at a time and continue to stir it. Do this about three or four times.

Afterwards, dip the cookies into the confectioners' coating, and then press the cookies into the candy canes. Set the cookies aside to allow them to set. Enjoy!

Peppermint Oatmeal Lace Cookies

Recipe Makes 36 cookies.
Prep Time: 15 minutes.
Cook Time: 10 minutes.

Ingredients:
1 cup oats
1 cup softened butter
½ cup crushed peppermint
2 tsp. peppermint extract
1 cup and 2 tbsp. confections' sugar
1 1/3 cup all-purpose flour
1 tsp. salt

Directions:
Begin by preheating your oven to 325 degrees Fahrenheit.

Next, beat together the first cup of confectioners' sugar with the butter to create a cream. Add the peppermint extract. Stir.

Next, whisk in the salt and the flour slowly. Fold the oats into the mixture, and add half of the peppermint candies into the created dough. Stir well.

Next, drop small balls of the dough onto a baking sheet, and press the cookies a little at the top. Bake the cookies for twelve minutes, and allow them to cool.

To the side, stir together the 2 tbsp. of confectioners' sugar with the other half of the peppermint candies. Dust this mixture overtop of the prepared cookies, and enjoy.

Festive Peppermint Bark Cookies

Recipe Makes 48 cookies.
Prep Time: 20 minutes.
Cook Time: 10 minutes.

Ingredients:
2 1/3 cups all-purpose flour
2 eggs
1 tsp. baking soda
1 tsp. vanilla
1 tsp. peppermint extract
½ cup softened butter
½ tsp. salt
½ tsp. red food coloring
½ cup vegetable shortening
1 cup brown sugar
1/3 cup white sugar
2 ¼ cup white chocolate chips
7 crushed peppermint candy canes

Directions:
Begin by preheating the oven to 350 degrees Fahrenheit.

Next, stir together flour, salt, and the baking soda in a small bowl.

To the side, beat together the vegetable shortening, butter, white sugar, and the brown sugar in a large bowl. Make sure to beat it until it's creamy. Next, add the vanilla, eggs, and the peppermint extract. Drop the red food coloring and continue to mix. Add the dry ingredients a little at a time, and continue to stir until the dough is completely smooth. Next, add the candy canes and the chocolate chips.

Nip off tablespoon amounts of the dough, and roll these pieces into balls. Place the balls on a baking sheet, and flatten them a bit with a glass.

Bake the cookies for ten minutes. Allow them to sit for a few minutes prior to cooling them on wire racks. Enjoy!

CHAPTER 3
HOLIDAY
Spice Cookies

Runaway Gingerbread Man Cookies

Recipe Makes 32 cookies.
Prep Time: 20 minutes.
Cook Time: 10 minutes.

Ingredients:
2 cups sifted flour
½ cup butter
½ cup molasses
1/3 cup sugar
1 egg yolk
½ tsp. baking powder
½ tsp. salt
1 tsp. cinnamon
½ tsp. baking soda
1 tsp. ginger
1 tsp. cloves
1 tsp. nutmeg

Directions:
Begin by mixing together the sugar and the butter until they're completely smooth. Add the egg yolk and the molasses to the mixture, and completely assimilate the ingredients.

To the side, stir together salt, baking powder, baking soda, flour, cinnamon, ginger, cloves, and the nutmeg. Add this dry mixture to the wet mixture, and stir completely. Cover the batter and allow the batter to cool in the refrigerator for one hour.

Next, preheat the oven to 350 degrees Fahrenheit. Roll out the dough on a floured surface, and cut the dough up utilizing a gingerbread man cookie cutter.

Place the cookies on a baking sheet with a few inches between them, and allow them to bake for ten minutes. Decorate or eat as-is afterwards!

Ginger Joyful Christmas Cookies

Recipe Makes 24 cookies.
Prep Time: 15 minutes.
Cook Time: 10 minutes.

Ingredients:
2 cups all-purpose flour
1 cup softened butter
2 tsp. ginger
1 cup sugar
1 egg
1 tsp. baking soda
½ tsp. cloves
1 tsp. cinnamon
1 tbsp. water
1/3 cup molasses
½ tsp. salt
2 tbsp. white sugar (for sprinkling)

Directions:
Begin by preheating the oven to 350 degrees Fahrenheit.

Next, stir together the cinnamon, cloves, salt, ginger, baking soda, and flour. Place this mixture to the side.

Next, stir together the first cup of sugar, butter, egg, water, and the molasses. Make sure to stir between each addition. Next, stir the dry mixture into the wet mixture slowly.

Roll the dough into small balls, and then roll the balls in the 2 tbsp. of white sugar for a coating. Place the cookies on a cookie sheet, and flatten them just a bit.

Bake the cookies in the oven for ten minutes. Afterwards, allow the cookies to cool and store them in a container. Enjoy throughout Christmas!

Perfection Pumpkin Cookies

Recipe Makes 36 cookies
Prep Time: 20 minutes
Cook Time: 20 minutes

Ingredients:
2 ¼ cups all-purpose flour
1 can pumpkin puree
1 tsp. baking powder
1 egg
1 tsp. vanilla
1 ½ cups white sugar
1 tsp. baking soda
2 tsp. cinnamon
½ tsp. nutmeg
1 tsp. cloves
½ cup softened butter
1 tsp. salt
1 tbsp. melted butter
1 tsp. vanilla (for drizzle)
3 tbsp. milk
2 cups confectioners' sugar

Directions:
Begin by preheating the oven to 350 degrees Fahrenheit.

In a small bowl, stir together the baking soda, the flour, the baking powder, the cinnamon, the nutmeg, the cloves, and the salt. Set this mixture to the side.

Next, in a large bowl, mix together the softened butter, the white sugar, the egg, the pumpkin puree, and the vanilla. Stir well. Add the dry ingredients, then, and stir until the mixture is completely assimilated.

Next, drop the cookies onto the cookie sheet, and flatten them a bit on the top. Bake the cookies for twenty minutes.

Next, make the glaze by mixing together the milk, the confectioners' sugar, the melted butter, and the vanilla. Note that you can add additional milk in order to create a consistency that will drizzle well over the cookies. Drizzle the mixture over the cookies, and enjoy!

Everything Nice Cinnamon Palmiers

Recipe Makes 24 cookies.
Prep Time: 20 minutes.
Cook Time: 15 minutes.

Ingredients:
2/3 cup white sugar
1 tsp. cinnamon
¼ tsp. cardamom
1 sheet of a thawed puff pastry
1 tbsp. melted butter
Water

Directions:
Begin by placing a quarter cup of the white sugar over a flat surface. Place the puff pastry overtop this sugar, and roll it into a 15 by 10 inch rectangle. Melt the butter, and brush this butter all over the puff pastry.

To the side, mix together the remaining sugar, cinnamon, and the cardamom, and sprinkle this mixture over the buttered puff pastry.

Next, roll the pastry in on itself from both directions, meeting the two rolls in the center. Place a bit of water on your fingertips, and dot the water in the very center, where the two rolls meet. Make sure that the rolls will not come apart. Next, allow the dough to refrigerate for fifteen minutes.

Preheat the oven to 375 degrees Fahrenheit.

Cut the pastry into ¼ inch slices. Arrange these slices on a baking sheet, one inch apart from each other. Bake the cinnamon slices in the oven for twelve minutes. Afterwards, allow them to cool, and enjoy!

Springerle Spiced Cookies

Recipe Makes 48 cookies.
Prep Time: 45 minutes.
Cook Time: 8 minutes.

Ingredients:
2 eggs
2 cups all-purpose flour
1 cup white sugar
¼ tsp. baking ammonia
1 tsp. lemon zest
¼ tsp. anise oil
2 tbsp. anise seeds

Directions:
Begin by beating together sugar, eggs, lemon peel, and the anise oil. The final mixture should be very thick.

To the side, blend together baking ammonia and the flour. Bring the egg and sugar mixture into the flour mixture very slowly, bits at a time, mixing between each addition. Cover the created dough with a towel and allow it to sit at room temperature for one and a half hours.

Next, create a ball from the fermented dough, and place it on a floured surface. Knead at the dough and then roll it out with a rolling pin.

Draw on the created dough to make springerle designs using toothpicks or a classic springerle mold- found on Amazon or at your local grocery store. Note that you can either create your own design by making indentations in the dough with toothpicks, or you can use the pre-made molds. Next cut around the designs with a knife. Place the towel over these cut frames, and allow them to stand at room temperature for twenty-four hours.

Next, preheat your oven to 325 degrees Fahrenheit. Grease the cookie sheet, and coat the cookie sheet with a single layer of the anise seeds.

Brush each of the back of the cookie dough frames with a bit of water. Place the cookie frames on the cookie sheet, and bake the cookies for eight minutes. Allow the cookies to cool, and allow them to be stored in an airtight location for a full two weeks prior to serving. Enjoy!

CHAPTER 4
HOLIDAY
No Bake Cookies

Lazy Days Grandma's Christmas Peanut Butter Fudge Balls

Recipe Makes 20 balls.
Prep Time: 20 minutes.
Cooke time: 0 minutes.

Ingredients:
1 ¼ cup peanut butter
2 cups confectioners' sugar
1/3 cup melted butter
2 tbsp. cocoa powder
1 tsp. vanilla extract
3 tbsp. marshmallow cream

Directions:
Begin by melting the butter. Mix the above ingredients together in a large bowl, and stir until smooth. Afterwards, form the dough into one-inch balls, allow them to sit out on a baking sheet— separate—for about one hour prior to refrigerating them—or freezing them— and enjoy!

Chubby Chocolate Rum Balls

Recipe Makes 48 cookies.
Prep Time: 45 minutes.
Cook Time: 0 minutes.

Ingredients:
1 ½ cups diced walnuts
3 ½ cups crushed vanilla wafers
1/3 cup unsweetened cocoa powder
1 cup confectioners' sugar
3 tbsp. corn syrup
½ cup rum

Directions:
Begin by stirring together the confectioners' sugar, nuts, cocoa powder, and the crushed vanilla wafers.

Afterwards, add the corn syrup and the rum slowly, stirring to completely assimilate the ingredients.

Portion the batter into 1-inch balls and roll them up, coating them with sugar. Place the balls in a container and allow them to sit in the refrigerator for a few days to completely administer the desired flavor.

Enjoy!

Bumbling Butterscotch Holiday Haystacks

Recipe Makes 60 cookies.
Prep Time: 20 minutes.
Cook Time: 0 minutes.

Ingredients:
1 ¼ cup peanut butter
¾ package of butterscotch chips
1 can chow mein noodles

Directions:
Begin by melting the butterscotch and the peanut butter together in a saucepan on the stovetop over low heat. After it's completely melted and completely mixed, pour this mixture over the chow mein noodles and stir well.

Afterwards, drop the noodles with the butterscotch and peanut butter coating onto wax paper one tablespoon at a time. Freeze the cookies for about four hours. Afterwards, store the cookies in a cool, dry location, and enjoy throughout the holidays.

A Cherry Occasion No-Bake Cookies

Recipe Makes 24 cookies.
Prep Time: 15 minutes.
Cook Time: 0 minutes.

Ingredients:

1 cup softened butter
1 tsp. vanilla
1 ¼ cup powdered sugar
½ cup chopped and drained maraschino cherries
2 cups oats
1 cup sweetened coconut
½ cup ground peanuts or ground almonds

Direction:

Bring together butter, sugar, cherries, vanilla, and the coconut. Stir well, and add the oats. When the mixture is completely assimilated, refrigerate the dough for three hours.

Afterwards, roll up the dough into one-inch balls. Roll these balls in the prepared, chopped peanuts or walnuts. Store these balls in a container in the refrigerator or freezer, and enjoy throughout the season!

Most Wonderful Time of the Year Coconut Snowballs

Recipe Makes 60 cookies.
Prep Time: 15 minutes.
Cook Time: 0 minutes.

Ingredients:
12 ounces white chocolate chips
2 tbsp. heavy cream
2 tbsp. bourbon
6 ounces ground almonds
1 ½ cup sweetened coconut flakes

Directions:
Begin by bringing the chocolate chips and the cream in a small bowl. Set this bowl over a pan of simmering—not boiling water—and stir the mixture until it's melted. Add the bourbon and the almonds at this time, and continue to stir. Spread this mixture in a baking pan, and allow it to chill for a full hour.

After an hour, slice the dough into one-inch pieces. Roll the squares into balls, and roll these balls in the sweetened coconut. Allow the balls to remain chilled, and enjoy as you please!

CHAPTER 5
HOLIDAY
Round-the-World Cookies

Rosy Rosenmunnar Christmas Cookies

Recipe Makes 72 cookies.
Prep Time: 40 minutes.
Cook Time: 15 minutes.

Ingredients:
2 ¼ cups sifted flour
1 cup softened butter
1/3 cup white sugar
½ cup raspberry fruit jam

Directions:
Begin by preheating the oven to 375 degrees Fahrenheit.

Next, stir together the softened butter and the sugar. Create a light texture. Next, add the sifted flour to the mixture and stir.

Formulate one-inch cookie balls from the batter and place them on baking sheets. Place a little implantation in the center of the cookie, and portion out the raspberry jam into the cookie holes.

Bake the cookies for fifteen minutes, and allow them to cool. Enjoy.

French Noelle Peppermint Meringue

Recipe Makes 48 Cookies.
Prep Time: 20 minutes.
Cook Time: 90 minutes.

Ingredients:
½ cup sugar
2 egg whites
¼ tsp. cream of tartar
2 crushed peppermint candy canes
¼ tsp. salt

Directions:
Begin by preheating your oven to 225 degrees Fahrenheit. Place large sheets of aluminum foil overtop of baking sheets to prepare for the coming cookies.

Next, in a large glass bowl, mix together the egg whites, cream of tartar, and salt. Create soft peaks. Next, add the crushed candy canes and sugar and continue to mix until you formulate stiff white peaks.

Drop spoonfuls of the created batter onto the baking sheets and allow them to bake for 90 minutes. After 90 minutes, shut off the oven and open the door so that it's ajar. Allow the meringues to sit on the oven rack until they're completely cooled. Afterwards, remove the meringues and store them in a covered container.

Cravin' Cranberry Christmas Biscotti

Recipe Makes 36 cookies.
Prep Time: 25 minutes.
Cook Time: 45 minutes.

Ingredients:
2 cups all-purpose flour
1/3 cup olive oil
1 cup white sugar
½ tsp. salt
1 tsp. baking powder
2 tsp. vanilla
½ cup dried cranberries
½ tsp. almond extract
1 ¾ cup pistachios
2 eggs

Directions:
Begin by preheating the oven to 300 degrees Fahrenheit.

Next, mix together the sugar and the oil. Add the almond extract, vanilla, and eggs, and beat the mixture until completely assimilated.

Next, add the flour, baking powder, and the salt gradually, stirring between each addition. Add the nuts and the cranberries, and mix these ingredients into the bowl by hand.

Next, divide the created dough into two equal halves. Formulate into 12 by 2 inch "strips" on a baking sheet. Bake the strips for thirty-five minutes. Afterwards, remove the strips from the oven, and allow them to cool for ten minutes to the side. During this time, reduce your oven's heat to 275 degrees Fahrenheit.

Next, slice up the strips into ¾ inch wide slices. Lay these strips out on the baking sheet, and bake them for an additional ten minutes. They should be completely dry. Allow them to cool, and enjoy!

Croatian Christmas Medenjaci Cookies

Recipe Makes 48 cookies.
Prep Time: 3 days.
Cook Time: 10 minutes.

Ingredients:
2 ½ cups all-purpose flour
2 ½ cups cake flour
½ cup whole wheat flour
1 cup butter
3 eggs
1 cup white sugar
1 cup honey
2 tsp. cinnamon
1 tsp. baking soda
½ tsp. cloves
1 tsp. nutmeg
½ tsp. ginger
12 quartered walnuts

Directions:
Begin by stirring together honey, sugar, and butter in a saucepan, allowing the butter to melt and the sugar to dissolve.

Allow this mixture to cool, afterwards, for a full ten minutes.

Next, mix together all the flours, baking soda, cloves, cinnamon, ginger, and the nutmeg in a small bowl. Add this mixture into the butter mixture, and stir until the mixture formulates soft dough.

Cover the saucepan with the complete dough creation with aluminum foil, and allow the mixture to ferment for three days.

Afterwards, preheat the oven to 375 degrees Fahrenheit. Divide the fermented dough into long, 2/3 inch wide ropes. Cut the strips into 2-inch long sections, and roll the dough into small balls. Place the balls on the baking sheets, and press the walnut portions into the tops of the cookies.

Bake the cookies for twelve minutes, and allow them to cool prior to serving.

Parisian Delight Chocolate Ganache Cookies

Recipe Makes 24 cookies.
Prep Time: 30 minutes.
Cook Time: 90 minutes.

Ingredients:
2 ¼ cups confectioners' sugar
3 egg whites
¼ cup white sugar
¼ tsp. cream of tartar
½ tsp. peppermint extract
1 package semisweet chocolate chips
1 cup heavy whipping cream
1 tsp. white sugar
1 crushed peppermint candy cane

Directions:
Begin by placing the rack of your oven at the very bottom and preheating the oven to 175 degrees Fahrenheit.

To the side, whisk the egg whites and the initial ¼ cup of white sugar in a double boiler over a simmering pot of water. After the ingredients are smooth, whisk in the peppermint extract and the cream of tartar. Continue to beat until it's foamy. Afterwards, add the confectioners' sugar into the mixture and beat well until the mixture creates stiff peaks.

Place the cookies on the baking sheet in one-tablespoon increments. Shape the cookies into "footballs" and allow them to cook for about one hour and thirty minutes in the oven. Next, allow them to cool.

To make the frosting, melt the chocolate chips in the double boiler over a simmering pot of water. The chocolate should completely melt. Afterwards, add the whipping cream and the final tsp. of white sugar, stirring between each addition.

Stir the mixture until it's thick, and dip each cookie into the created ganache. Sprinkle the cookies with the crushed peppermint, and allow them to cool and set prior to enjoying.

Merry Milano Cookies

Recipe Makes 40 Cookies.
Prep Time: 15 minutes.
Cook Time: 10 minutes.

Ingredients:
1 ½ tsp. vanilla extract
½ cup softened butter
½ cup vegetable shortening
2 ¼ cups all-purpose flour
1 cup confectioners' sugar
½ tsp. almond extract
3 tbsp. water
1 egg
½ tsp. salt
1 ¼ cup chocolate chips

Directions:
Begin by preheating the oven to 375 degrees Fahrenheit.

Next, beat together the shortening and the butter. Add the confectioners' sugar, egg, water, vanilla, and almond extract. After you've completely mixed the above, add the salt and the flour. Add the chocolate chips into the dough, and stir well.

Drop the cookies onto a baking sheet, and allow the cookies to bake for nine minutes. Enjoy!

Chipper Christmas Coconut Macaroons

Recipe Makes 15 cookies.
Prep Time: 15 minutes.
Cook Time: 5 minutes.

Ingredients:
2 ¼ cups white sugar
2 cups oats
½ cup softened butter
1 cup shredded coconut
½ cup milk
¼ cup cocoa powder

Directions:
Begin by mixing together the oats, cocoa powder, and the coconut together in a small bowl.

Bring together butter, sugar, and milk in a saucepan, and heat the ingredients over low heat, stirring occasionally. After the mixture has completely mixed, take it off the heat, and add the prepared oat mixture.

After you've stirred completely, drop the batter onto a baking sheet, and allow the cookies to set at room temperature prior to enjoying.

German Spice Lebkuchen Cookies

Recipe Makes 36 cookies.
Prep Time: 24 hours.
Cook Time: 15 minutes.

Ingredients:
2 eggs
2 cups almonds
1 cup brown sugar
1 cup honey
1/3 cup blackstrap molasses
1 cup dried and chopped apricots
8 pitted and chopped dried dates
4 1/3 cups all-purpose flour
1 tbsp. cinnamon
2 tsp. grated orange zest
2 tsp. ginger
1 tsp. grated lemon zest
1 ½ tsp. baking powder
1 tsp. cloves
1 tsp. cardamom
1 tsp. cloves
½ tsp. salt
2 tbsp. whole milk
1 cup confectioners' sugar
1 tsp. lemon zest

Directions:

Begin by placing almonds in a bowl and covering the almonds in boiling water. Allow the almonds to sit in the water for two minutes prior to draining them. Now, rinse them out with cold water and drain them once more. Pat them dry and completely remove the almond skin.

Next, portion half of the above almonds in a food processor. Chop them until they're fine. Afterwards, add the dates and the apricots and chop them together. To the side, combine together cinnamon, ginger, flour, baking powder, cardamom, cloves, and salt. Stir well.

Mix together brown sugar, eggs, honey, molasses, almond extract, water, orange zest, and 1 tsp. of lemon zest; stir this mixture until it's smooth. Add the created almond and apricot mixture to this mixture, and stir well.

Next, add the dry flour mixture into the dough, and stir until the dough is completely smooth. Cover this dough with aluminum foil or plastic wrap, and allow the dough to refrigerate over night.

Preheat your oven to 350 degrees Fahrenheit.

Roll out the above dough on a floured surface, and cut out the cookies with a cookie cutter. Place the cookies on a cookie sheet, and press three of the non-processed almonds into each cookie.

Bake the cookies for twelve minutes, and allow them to cool.

To the side, mix together the remaining confectioners' sugar, the tsp. of lemon zest, and the milk. Stir well until it's smooth, and brush this mixture over the still-warm cookies. Enjoy!

Goodies Gingerbread Biscotti

Recipe Makes 48 cookies.
Prep Time: 25 minutes.
Cook Time: 40 minutes.

Ingredients:
1/3 cup vegetable oil
1 ¼ cup white sugar
1/3 cup molasses
3 eggs
1 cup whole wheat flour
2 cups all-purpose flour
1 ½ tbsp. ginger
1 tbsp. baking powder
1 tbsp. cinnamon
½ tsp. nutmeg
¼ tsp. cloves

Directions:
Begin by preheating your oven to 375 degrees Fahrenheit.

Next, mix together eggs, oil, sugar, and the molasses in a large bowl.

To the side, in a different bowl, mix together spices, baking powder, and the flours. Combine the wet ingredients with the dry ingredients, and stir well.

Afterwards, divide the dough into two equal portions. Shape the dough into a roll the very length of a normal cookie. Place these rolls on your baking sheet, and flatten the dough into a half-inch thickness.

Next, bake the biscotti for twenty-five minutes in the preheated oven.

After the cookies are cool to the touch, cut the cookies into half inch thick slices. Place these slices on the cookie sheet once more, and bake them for an additional five minutes on each side. They should be crisp and delicious!